YOUR KNOWLEDGE HAS VALUE

Alexander Borodin

The Significance of the Athenian Model in revealing the fundamental limits and opportunities of democratic self-governance

Important lessons to be learnt from Athenian democracy

GRIN Verlag

Bibliografische Information der Deutschen Nationalbibliothek:

Die Deutsche Bibliothek verzeichnet diese Publikation in der Deutschen National-
bibliografie; detaillierte bibliografische Daten sind im Internet über http://dnb.d-
nb.de/ abrufbar.

Imprint:

Copyright © 2012 GRIN Verlag GmbH
Druck und Bindung: Books on Demand GmbH, Norderstedt Germany
ISBN: 978-3-656-26317-3

This book at GRIN:

http://www.grin.com/en/e-book/199955/the-significance-of-the-athenian-model-
in-revealing-the-fundamental-limits

GRIN - Your knowledge has value

Der GRIN Verlag publiziert seit 1998 wissenschaftliche Arbeiten von Studenten, Hochschullehrern und anderen Akademikern als eBook und gedrucktes Buch. Die Verlagswebsite www.grin.com ist die ideale Plattform zur Veröffentlichung von Hausarbeiten, Abschlussarbeiten, wissenschaftlichen Aufsätzen, Dissertationen und Fachbüchern.

Visit us on the internet:

http://www.grin.com/

http://www.facebook.com/grincom

http://www.twitter.com/grin_com

The Significance of the Athenian Model

In revealing the fundamental limits and

Opportunities of democratic self-governance

Alexander Borodin

University of Essex

GV 100: Introduction to Politics

25th of January, 2012

In many ways Athenian assembly democracy constitutes a genuine as well as extreme model in democratic thought. This has to do on the one hand with its remarkable institutional features and on the other hand with its extensive practices of public participation. In what will follow, we should therefore at first look at the structure and the interrelations of the key organs of the Athenian system as a form of government. Our understanding of the mechanisms of these institutions will serve us as a basis to enquire critically into their actual performance as well as their significance for Athenian democracy as a whole. Investigating the principles behind the institutions such as selection by lot, very short periods of office or reliance on public opinion will then allow us to reflect on their implications for modern discourse on democratic ideas. It is my intention to illustrate how the Athenian system and particularly the broad public deliberation it relied on, exemplifies the necessary criteria which have to be achieved in order to strengthen rather than to undermine democracy. Whereas the

Athenian model needs to be limited in some respects, for instance to avoid violations of the rule of law, it has to be furthered in other respects such as the enlightenment of the wide public.

Initiating a discussion on the legacy of the Athenian democracy, one has to acknowledge that a thorough understanding of its inner structure and mechanisms is indispensable in order to enable us to identify its positive as well as negative facets. If we refer most basically to the "demos" (p.32, Evans, 2010) or citizenry of the Athenian democracy, we should be aware that this comprises solely all male citizens above the age of 20 who are subdivided into 10 tribes based on their local residence. All other groups, most notably women, people of non-Athenian descent and slaves didn't belong to the citizenry and accordingly had no right to participate in the Assembly or any other public arenas (Ober, 2008). Accordingly, they were excluded from any function or decision-making role. In spite of this considerable exclusion it is crucial to note that there has been no "property qualification for the enjoyment of political rights" (Rhodes, 2004). The sole criterion to become a citizen was to have Athenian parents and it didn't matter for example which social class one belonged to. Thus, the citizenry which made a fifth of the total population was entitled and publicly encouraged to participate in the Assembly which took place at a minimum of 40 occasions per year. A striking feature of the Athenian Assembly was that it required a total of 6000 voters to ratify a decision made by the people. This number bears at least two implications. The first is that a decision wouldn't be ratified if not enough people gathered to the assembly which ensured that the presence of a considerable number of people to represent different standpoints and avoid the dominance of one faction. In addition, this particular number of 6000 participants entails that there has been rarely or not at all less people present. In fact, the high degree of participation was rooted in the very idea of this form of government, which is direct democracy. On the political sphere

2

there was no distinction between government and the public, they both formed one inextricable unit in which citizens could in a process of interactive deliberation make use of their role as self-governors. Ideally, the will of the people and not the will of a marginal minority as aristocrats or oligarchs should constitute each decision the Assembly arrived to. But how did the Assembly select matters that were debated in these sessions, which institution was responsible for raising them? This was clearly the task of the Council of 500 also called the "Boule" (p. 28, Thorley, 2004) which worked as the executive body of the Athenian government. Its principal function was to "prepare the agenda for the meeting of the Assembly" (p.31, Hansen, 1999) by means of draft proposals and as such it exerted a significant influence on the content of the discussions held in the Assembly. Likewise, this organ received all foreign embassies, supervised financial and military matters and could even act as a court. By implementing the policy which was decided upon by the Assembly, the Boule was "crucial to the working of the whole new democratic system" (p.31, Hansen, 1999). In the face of the huge importance of the Council of 500, it is not surprising that its membership was highly restricted by age, demos and property qualification even though over the course of the 4th century the latter criterion was dismissed. The annual change of its entire membership and the one-day office of its president were based upon the democratic principles of rotation, distribution and power share. The judicial sphere was also dominated by ordinary citizens who were appointed by lot from a pool of 6000 people to guide a particular trial. Thus, the People's law courts were likewise run by popular consensus rather than the judgement of official experts. In the course of this work, we will elaborate on this reliance on public opinion which evidently constitutes a decisive cornerstone of the Athenian system of government. As we have now gained an understanding of the overall structure of the crucial institutions of Athenian democracy, we can now adapt a deeper perspective on the performance of these cornerstones and their relation to democratic principles.

How do these organs relate to democracy, do they strengthen or undermine Athenian democracy and what was their contribution to the integrity of the system as a whole? Let us begin with a reflection on what one may characterize as the epitome of Athenian democracy, the Assembly. Perhaps the most remarkable characteristic of the Athenian assembly was that it had no exclusive connotations regarding property or class belonging. Any given Athenian citizen of the estimated total of 30000 could come to the Assembly, occupy his mind with the issues presented, participate directly in the following discussion and ultimately vote on the particular concern which was decided by a simple majority rule. Thus, the Assembly was the principal organ that constituted Athenian primary democracy since the participants' decision directly determined the outcome of the matter in question. What was the distinctive feature about this form of public deliberation is the participants' extreme involvement in a majority of the debated issues. The decisions made by the Assembly were very likely to have financial, social and at times even existential effects on the citizens depending on the magnitude of the decision. Whether starting a military campaign, changes in taxation or restrictions to the citizenship, all these generally public, not private matters decisively shaped the private life of the ordinary people. This immediateness of the voting process is one explanation for the encouraging feeling of involvement of the Athenian citizens. This high degree of civic participation was an indispensable condition for the functioning of the Assembly and Athenian democracy as a whole. Despite of the apparent democratic character of this institution, it had undeniable limits due to the ratio of available time and the amount of people engaging in it. On Stockwell's account (p.22, Stockwell, 2011) the "sheer size of these gatherings prohibited a robust exchange of views". Participation was theoretically open to anyone, but in reality exclusive to "just a few (elite, wealthy and well-educated) citizens". However, this objection could only be validated if a majority was inexperienced regarding such public interactions and would show as a result significant sensitivity to the "superior mastery of both rhetoric and technical matters" (p. 162, Ober, 2008) of an elite minority.

4

Instead, it was institutionally guaranteed most notably by means of the Council of 500 and the People's law courts that a high percentage of the Assemblymen necessarily gained at least once in their life a personal insight in the functioning of these organs, their agenda and the social networks they comprised. One might still insist that these offices weren't sufficient to equip the ordinary Athenian citizens with a form of expertise that was necessary in dealing with issues debated in the Assembly. This argument would severely undermine the self-governing approach of the Athenians under the condition that people voted by secret ballot, but since even the most inexperienced and ignorant Athenians could consult the arguments put forward by the supposedly more informed speakers, they could use their own reason to reflect on them and form an own conclusion. Thus, the response of such an individual "was in turn conditioned by his own monitoring of the reactions of those in his extensive network whom he knew to be particularly expert" (p.163, Ober, 2008). An ignorant participant of the Assembly could therefore identify himself with a particular argument because of the authority the person exerted over him or for the pure merit of the argument in the eyes of the citizen. Even though the Athenian form of government at its heart was grounded on the principle of "isonomia" (p.35, Roberts, 1994), which alludes to the equal opportunity to participate in politics, it incontrovertibly "encompassed in practice various inequalities" such as "lack of leisure and lack of resources" (p. 193, Sinclair, 1988). Thus, it remains doubtful whether true "effective participation" (p.37, Dahl, 1998) without discrimination against minorities was feasible in the Athenian system and is feasible at all. In conclusion, we should recall the extraordinary circumstances of spontaneity and unpredictability by which the Assembly meetings were marked combined with a general emphasis on mutual deliberation between the Athenian citizens that fundamentally conflict with the critical notion of the voting process as just "rubber-stamp mechanisms" (p.162, Ober, 2008). The effectiveness of the Athenian system resulted above all from "its practical form of civic education" (p. 273, Ober, 2008) which was mainly achieved through the integrative character of governance and the socialisation each Athenian underwent by participating in public rituals and ceremonies. After assessing the importance of the Assembly as the legislative and executive body of the Athenian system, it follows logically to sharpen the look at the judicial practises within the People's law courts and their contribution to Athenian democracy.

The mechanisms and practises behind the popular law courts serve our enterprise in the way that their evaluation exemplifies to a great extent both the essential assets and the undeniable flaws of Athenian self-governance. First of all the selection of jurors each year by selection from a "pool of 6000" (p.99, Stockton, 1990) of Athenian citizens aged more than 30 mirrored the idea of egalitarian, public participation in crucial spheres of governance. The underlying assumption is that a group great in number could form in its totality a reasonable and right decision and thus enforcing the rule of law. The evident advantage of this method was the virtual exclusion of bribery and corruption of the jury whose composition was under constant change. The highly complex "method of allotment of jurors made it impossible for an orator to predict who would be judging his case" (p.121, Stockton, 1990) assured at the same time that there was no predominant group represented that could base their judgements on "favour or enmity" rather than on "the laws and decrees passed by the Assembly and the Boule" (p. 37, Thorley, 2004). Even though this method was very democratic in its origin and was likely to guarantee impartiality, its outcome could be decided comparably to an Assembly meeting by an excellent rhetorical performance of one of the participants. As a result professional speech-writers designed the speeches so that they were particularly appealing to the jury (p. 114, Cohen and Gagarin, 2005). Accordingly, such common techniques to influence the jury entailed that the constitutional rule of law was repeatedly violated and replaced by popular and unreflecting decisions. The decision could thus be supported by an overwhelming majority, but at the same time be against the constitution of the state. This paradox lies at the

6

heart of democratic thought which if practiced in such a pure and unrestricted way can bear self-undermining implications for the system as a form of government. If public consensus is rested on over-hasty decisions driven my populist movement rather than rational deliberation and "rises above the law" (p. 12, Woodruff, 2006), then democracy inevitably succumbs to a tyranny of the majority, which "kills freedom as dead as any other form of tyranny" (p. 12, Woodruff, 2006). It is between these dimensions, democratic thought faces its toughest challenge.

Do governmental positions necessitate expertise or is conversely a group of amateurs perfectly entitled to fulfil these positions? Clearly, it occurs throughout the whole Athenian model in principle that collective, although amateurish deliberation on crucial public matters is furthered. The Athenians' trust in "reasoning without knowledge" (p.171, Woodruff, 2006) was also reflected in the crucial organ, the Council of 500, whose members were chosen by lot and could stay in office for one year without the possibility of remaining in office. Perhaps the most democratically remarkable mechanism in the Boule was the "selection by lot of the president on a daily basis" (p.32, Sinclair) which empowered a majority of its members to exercise the leading role of a chairman completely on their own. The underlying assumption is that self-governance through the people won't be possible if professionally trained experts remain in charge over a long period of time. However, at this stage we have to enquire into the practicability of such a limitless form of democracy. Doesn't this Athenian experiment imply despite its great merits of accountability and transparency, severe instability and even chaos? According to Josiah Ober (Ober, 2008) on the contrary "the mediating and integrative power of communication between citizens" was the key to the relative stability of Athenian democracy. Let us then imagine a society without these prerequisites of almost socialised interest and engagement in public matters, fulfilling the roles of the very same arenas such as the Boule, the Law Courts or the Assembly, what would necessarily follow? Such a system is condemned to fail and shortly succumb in despotic rule. What we now begin to realise is that the success of a form of government which is directly executed and enforced by its citizenry, is inextricably linked to the social and public interaction of this citizenry. In other words the values and principles this society is grounded on, will determine the character and success of the citizens' self-governance. That's why not the doubtless highly democratic institutions of the Athenian system were the distinguishing factor for its persistence, but rather the "civic culture" (p.7, Monoson, 2000) that shaped them. At its core Athenian citizenship covered not only the political sphere of active participation in the various democratic institutions, but was mainly a "matter of the ritualized performance of a cluster of cultural practices that reach both into private and public life" (p.6, Monoson, 2000). At this stage, it appears necessary to remind us that despite all these positive facets of Athenian civic culture and its strengthening implications for democracy, this occurred under the presence of gender inequality, xenophobia, imperialism, and slavery" (p.8, Monoson, 2000) and couldn't even exist without these negative sights.

Applying the inferences we drew from the strengths and weaknesses of Athenian democracy in a broader context, empowers us to recognize that there are certain indispensable restrictions a democratic form of government requires. Direct democracy as witnessed in the Athenian experiment presupposes to a great extent a public wide "enlightened understanding" (p.37, Dahl, 1998) at least concerning the key policies on the agenda and works best if citizens can gain a true insight in the mechanisms and workings of government. What the Athenian experiment of direct democracy vividly expounds is that a genuine democratic system almost naturally conflicts with the realisation of good government (Zakaria, 2007). Let us elaborate, for instance, on stability and continuity as key characteristics of a good government and look

8

at its realisation in the Athenian model or any other form of direct democracy. As Assembly meetings, court trials and other comparable public arenas are under permanent change and rotation in their composition and structure, they further the complete opposite of continuity. For the Athenian system one has to remark that this wasn't even the principal goal of these procedures which was above all self-governance by and through the citizenship. Thus, Athenians seemed to sacrifice continuity for inherent self-governance, but are these two concepts genuine, perhaps radical democracy and good government really mutually exclusive? At this point, one has to stress the narrow correlation between these two ideals which however necessitates certain preconditions we can find in a basic form in Athenian democracy. Above all, a system that relies on non-expert opinion requires an equal and open access to useful knowledge and information as well as the possible consequences of certain policies. One way of fulfilling this condition is to encourage and further social interaction in private and public arenas and thus to enable its citizens to gain a broad understanding of important matters. Another vital point is to allow decisions especially the crucial ones to be verified and thought through unlike it was handled in the Athenian law courts and assemblies where time pressure entailed that decisions had often to be made on the same day which lead to a greater quantity of emotionally driven decisions. At the same, a concrete time limit has to be set in order to avoid endless deliberation and indecision. In my view, the Athenian experiment offers a radical example of civic involvement in all public matters, but this doesn't mean that this model cannot serve as an example for modern political debates. This example of what one may consider a pure or genuine democracy as the immediate governance by the people illustrates the most desirable as well as the most feared facets of the rule of the people. Thus, we might infer that democracy in its pure manner requires an underlying vibrant civic culture (Ober, 2008) as well as strict regulations regarding the enforcement of the rule of law. Yet, these necessities to limit democracy don't undermine at any rate direct democracy as a feasible alternative to the nowadays widely established representative democracy.

9

As we have seen in the course of this work, the ancient Athenian system propelled fundamentally democratic principles, such as public wide engagement in political decision making, free and open discourse on public matters or election by majority vote. Contrary to common assumption the Athenian practices, in particular its civic culture and trust in the common sense of its citizens, rather than its institutional features can serve as a model for contemporary democratic thought. The radical model of democracy in Athens reveals both the most fundamental limits of democracy in form of unreflecting and unlawful mass behaviour, as well as its great merits which can arise from extensive public discourse and a whole culture of collective self-governance.

Word Count: 3083

Bibliography

Books:

Ricardo Blaub and John Schwarzmantel, eds. Democracy: A Reader (Edinburgh: Edinburgh University Press, 2001)

David J. Cohen and Michael Gagarin, The Cambridge companion to ancient Greek law (New York: Cambridge University Press, 2005)

Robert A. Dahl, Democracy and Its Critics (New Haven, Conn.: Yale University Press, 1989)

Robert A. Dahl, On Democracy (New Haven, Conn.: Yale University Press, 1998)

Nancy Evans, Civic Rites: democracy and religion in ancient Athens (Berkeley : University of California Press, c2010)

Mogens H. Hansen, The Athenian democracy in the age of Demosthenes: structure, principles, and ideology (London: Bristol Classic Press, 1999)

David Held, Models of Democracy, 3rd edn. (Cambridge: Polity, 2006)

Sanford Lakoff, Democracy: History, Theory, Practice (Boulder, Col: Westview Press, 1996)

Iain M. Mackenzie, Politics key concepts in philosophy (London: Continuum, c2009)

Sara S. Monoson, Plato's Democratic Entanglements : Athenian Politics and the Practice of Philosophy (Princeton, N.J. : Princeton University Press, c2000)

Josiah Ober, Democracy and knowledge: innovation and learning in classical Athens (Princeton, N.J.; Woodstock: Princeton University Press, c2008)

Robin Osborne, Athens and Athenian democracy (New York: Cambridge University Press, 2010)

Kurt A. Raaflaub, Origins of democracy in ancient Greece (Berkeley: University of California Press, c2007)

Jennifer T. Roberts, Athens on trial: the antidemocratic tradition in Western thought (Princeton, N.J.: Princeton University Press, c1994)

Eric W. Robinson, Ancient Greek democracy readings and sources (Malden, Mass.: Blackwell Publishing, 2004)

Christopher Rocco, Tradegy and enlightenment: Athenian political thought and dilemmas of modernity (Berkeley: University of California Press, c1997)

Loren J.Samons, What's Wrong with Democracy? : From Athenian Practice to American Worship (University of California Press, 2004)

R. K. Sinclair, Democracy and participation in Athens (Cambridge: Cambridge University Press, 1988)

Stephen Stockwell, The secret history of democracy (Basingstoke: Palgrave Macmillan, 2011)

David Stockton, the classical Athenian democracy, (Oxford : Oxford University Press, 1990)

John Thorley, Athenian Democracy (Abingdon : Routledge, 2004, 2nd ed)

Stephen Tracy, Athenian democracy in transition: Attic letter-cutters of 340 to 290 B.C. (Berkeley: University of California Press, c1995)

Paul Woodruff, First democracy the challenge of an ancient idea (New York: Oxford University Press, 2006)

Fareed Zakaria, The Future of Freedom: Illiberal Democracy at Home and Abroad, 2nd edn. (New York, N.Y.: W.W. Norton, 2007)